AYRSHIRE
THEN & NOW
IN COLOUR

DANE LOVE

The
History
Press

First published in 2012

The History Press
The Mill, Brimscombe Port
Stroud, Gloucestershire, GL5 2QG
www.thehistorypress.co.uk

British Library Cataloguing in Publication Data.
A catalogue record for this book is available from the British Library.

ISBN 978 0 7524 7478 6

Typesetting and origination by The History Press
Manufactring managed by Jellyfish Print Solutions Ltd
Printed in India.

CONTENTS

ACKNOWLEDGEMENTS

The author would like to thank the Burns Monument Centre, Kilmarnock, for the supply of some original illustrations used in this book. All other old images and all of the modern pictures are from the author's collection.

ABOUT THE AUTHOR

Dane Love has written extensively on the history and heritage of Ayrshire in particular, and on Scottish subjects in general. He was born in Cumnock and now lives in the countryside near Auchinleck, with his wife and two children. He is the Honorary Secretary of the Scottish Covenanter Memorials Association. Among his more popular books are *Scottish Covenanter Stories*, *Scottish Ghosts*, *The Covenanter Encyclopaedia*, *Scottish Kirkyards*, and various other titles. He has written widely on Ayrshire places in books such as *Lost Ayrshire*, *Ayrshire – Discovering a County*, *Legendary Ayrshire*, as well as histories of various towns and villages. *Ayr Then and Now* is also available from The History Press. When not writing or researching, he works as a principal teacher at Irvine Royal Academy.

INTRODUCTION

The county of Ayrshire lies on the south-western corner of Scotland, a great arc sweeping around the Firth of Clyde. In general, the land rises to the north, east and south, the central stretch comprising of rolling countryside, famous for its Ayrshire cattle and farming. The periphery is surrounded by tall hills, or else wide moorlands, so that the county is separated from the rest of Scotland somewhat, resulting in a distinctive style of architecture, language and culture.

Apart from agriculture, Ayrshire has been well known over the centuries for its coalfields, though no deep mining remains today, its golf courses, including famous links courses such as Royal Troon, Old Prestwick and Turnberry, and its associations with the great bard Robert Burns.

The principal towns of the county are Ayr, Irvine and Kilmarnock, each of which is distinctive in its own right. The county town, Ayr, was always more of an administrative centre, rather than an industrial one, and had the added bonus of a wide sandy beach, beloved of holidaymakers, and a busy port. Irvine was a small burgh until it was developed as one of Scotland's 'new towns', creating a large sprawling community. Kilmarnock was always the more industrial of Ayrshire's large towns, famed in the past for its Johnnie Walker whisky, carpets, shoes, railway engines and water valves, to name but a few of the many industries carried on there.

The mention of holidaymakers brings to mind the tradition of going 'doon the watter' from Glasgow and other large Clydeside communities. The coastal resorts of Largs, Saltcoats, Prestwick, Troon, Ayr and Girvan catered for this trade for over a century, until the advent of cheap flights and guaranteed sun saw the tourists head for warmer climes. Nevertheless, breaks by the coast are still popular, the numerous caravan sites and holiday homes testifying to this.

Inland, the rural communities of Beith, Stewarton, Darvel, Cumnock, Dalmellington, and many other towns and villages, all had their own traditions and local industries. Beith was a centre for furniture making, Stewarton for bonnets, Darvel for lace, Cumnock for snuff-boxes and Dalmellington for iron. All of these traditional industries have gone, but today these communities all continue to exist, changing to suit modern society.

Sons of Ayrshire are numerous, and in addition to Burns, one must mention famous folk such as James Boswell, Sir Alexander Fleming, John Loudoun MacAdam and James Keir Hardie. Other sons of the county have travelled the world, making their mark abroad, such as Sir Thomas MakDougall Brisbane, James MacCosh and Robert Dunsmuir.

This book takes a look at most Ayrshire towns and villages, with pictures old and new. Unfortunately, not every community could be included, but there is certainly enough to whet the appetite of those interested in the story of the county. I hope you enjoy looking at how the communities have changed, or even stayed the same, over the years, every bit as much as I did.

Dane Love, 2012

ARDROSSAN

THE TOWN OF Ardrossan is a comparatively new place, compared with many of Ayrshire's ancient communities. It was established by the 12th Earl of Eglinton in 1806 as a new port on the Firth of Clyde, located below the ancient castle of Ardrossan. A grid of streets was laid out to the west of the Castle Hill, and a rather fine crescent of large villas to the south, overlooking the sandy bay. The streets were wide and grand, such as Princes Street (seen here). This runs approximately north-west to south-east, across the headland. To the right, the main Glasgow Street was to form the principal shopping area. The gates are for the level crossing here, where the railway crosses the street on its way to the harbour station. The station is to the right.

THE STATION IS still in use, but the large station building has been demolished, its site occupied by the red brick Michael Lynch Centre for Enterprise. Level crossings are today more obvious, with flashing lights and various signs, but one would think that the old gates would be safer. Beyond the enterprise centre the original buildings survive, still occupied by various shops. To the left, the former signal box for the crossing has been demolished, allowing a view of the Phoenix Gallery. The three-storey building behind it is Prince Albert House. The old terrace of shops and flats beyond remain, hidden in the image by the crossing lights. At the end of the row is the former Town Hall of 1856. The white buildings at the end of the street are modern flats built overlooking the marina, located in the old Eglinton Dock.

AUCHINLECK

IT WAS ALEXANDER BOSWELL, Lord Auchinleck, who laid out the present core of the village of Auchinleck in 1756. There was a fashion for creating planned villages across Scotland at the time, and Auchinleck was redesigned in the eighteenth century. His son, the famous diarist James Boswell, is buried in the Boswell Mausoleum here. The old village, with its ancient church, was rebuilt on a cruciform plan, with a long Main Street leading from the old mill to Templetown. This view shows the old Toll House on the left, with Mauchline Road disappearing into the distance. Halfway along is the oldest cottage surviving in the village – Dunbar – erected

in 1725. On the right is Campbell Place, which originally had seven houses and two shops. Beyond are the better houses of the village, home to people such as William Wilson, who owned a large sawmilling company which operated in the village for years.

THE OLD TOLL was demolished and replaced in 1915 by the double-storey Co-operative building, the upper floor of which had a hall, used by various community groups. It is now the office of a bus company. Campbell Place survives, now with only one commercial premise – the Corner Café – occupying it, along with housing. Old Dunbar cottage still remains, the thatch of 1921 replaced by slates. The parish church of 1838 (extended 1894) stands next to the old kirk, and the Boswell Arms inn of 1766 is prominent at the crossroads. Auchinleck still has its long Main Street, though many of the older buildings have gone. The old core is surrounded by council houses, built to replace the old miners' rows which littered the moors to the east. No coal mines survive, but the old winding gear of Highhouse Colliery still rises above the houses.

AYR

THE COUNTY TOWN, Ayr stands at the mouth of the river of that name. It was established around 1197 by William I, when he built his 'New Castle upon the Ayr'. The castle has long gone, but the town grew in importance over the centuries, and remains the most populous in the county. This old view shows the south-east end of High Street, looking towards the Wallace Tower, erected in 1833 on the site of a much older tower. Built to commemorate Sir William Wallace, the Scots patriot who was active in the town in the thirteenth century, it has a statue of him in a niche. The High Street was the busy shopping and commercial centre of the town, with places such as the Ayr Arms Hotel on the left, one of many hostelries that formerly existed within it. The trams operated in Ayr from 1901 until 1931.

THE WALLACE TOWER still dominates the High Street, the principal shopping area in the town. Virtually every commercial premise has changed since the old image was taken, apart from the Tam o' Shanter Inn, located to the right of the photographer, and still sporting a thatched roof. On the left, the old Ayr Arms has been rebuilt internally, forming part of the Kyle shopping centre, its entrance a traditional stone façade that fits well with the rest of the street. The trams have gone, and the street is closed to traffic apart from disabled drivers and buses. One of the main differences in the images is the inclusion of the Town Hall steeple in the new picture. This dates from 1827-32, so must have been removed from the old image for some reason. This end of the High Street is now the busiest part of the town.

BALLANTRAE

AN OLD GLASS negative of Ballantrae shows the corner of Main Street. On the right is the village post office. The ornate spire (with clock) on the parish church dates from 1891 but the rest of the building dates from 1819. Robert Burns' nephew was the minister here at one time. This part of the village was originally occupied by people associated with the land, whereas down by the little harbour was another community occupied by fishermen. Ballantrae was established in 1617 when the king agreed that the parish church could be relocated here from its inland location. The harbour pier was rebuilt in 1847, and at one time attracted pleasure steamers. Behind the railings to the left is the old kirkyard, where the older church stood. The Kennedy aisle, dating from around 1601, is still there. It commemorates Gilbert Kennedy, who was 'slain in feudal conflict'.

THE OLD THATCHED cottage in the centre of the old image has been rebuilt with a slate roof over an upper floor. At the right-hand end of the same row of houses is the King's Arms

Hotel, a busy inn, built in 1770 using stones acquired from nearby Ardstinchar Castle. Only gaunt remains of this tower survive, at one time playing host to Mary Queen of Scots. The busy main road still passes through the street, the traffic having to slow down as it takes the sharp corner at the former post office, now Thistles Tearoom. The shop next door is now just a cottage, called Corrie. The post office is now located at the opposite end of the Main Street, within the convenience store. The old harbour survives, but there are no steamers calling here now – just a few small pleasure craft make it home.

BARR

LOOKING OVER THE Water of Gregg, this postcard view shows the village of Barr. On the right, behind the stone wall with railings, is Barr Primary School, and Changue Road continued down by the side of the river to the junction of Glengennet Road, formerly Hill Street. The houses angling up the hill to the right are located in this road. The double-storey building, with the windows surrounds picked out in black, is the King's Arms Hotel, located in Stinchar Road. This was erected around 1800 as a coaching inn. Beyond it is the old kirkyard, where Covenanter graves can be found. The church with the clock tower was the Free Church, known as Kirk Angus, built in 1892 to plans by Alexander Petrie. Not visible in the picture is the parish church of 1878 and the village institute of 1913.

THE SPOT WHERE the photographer was standing in the old image is now part of the modern housing estate known as The Clachan, built on the south side of the stream. Unfortunately trees alongside the riverbank prevent the same view being obtained, but this image was taken from the footbridge across the Water of Gregg. The King's Arms Hotel still survives, offering food and accommodation, but the little cottage across the water from it has gone. The Free Church still stands, but it has been converted into a house, hidden by the trees. It closed as a church in 1987, the congregation joining the parish church. The primary school survives, with around thirty pupils in total, including the nursery class. Much of the surrounding countryside has been planted with trees, and the forests offer numerous walks and cycle routes.

BARRHILL

LOCATED REMOTELY ON the moors of south Ayrshire, the village of Barrhill grew up at the junction of the Cross Water with the Duisk River. Little more than two lines of traditional Ayrshire houses looking at each other across the street, the village had some importance as a small market centre with a railway station on the Ayr to Stranraer line. A market was held here for many years, popular for the sale of sheep, for which the moors were ideally suited. The parish church was erected at the west end of the village in 1887, the tower visible above the trees. This view was taken from the south-eastern end of Main Street. Hidden by the houses was the United Free Church, and near to it was the old smiddy. In addition, the heather-clad moors were popular for grouse-shooting, and a number of shooting lodges were built around the village.

THE VILLAGE STREET remains much the same, but the village is quieter, its remoteness being more of a problem in the modern age. The parish church has closed, and services are only held once a month in the village hall. The village retains its pub, known as The Trout, and a local shop. The local school has a roll of around twenty, from a population of about 350. The station survives, being mentioned in Dorothy L. Sayers' *Five Red Herrings*. The grouse moors are fewer now, much of the countryside around being afforested. One industry in the village is the manufacture of pre-cast concrete components, used in the building trade. Around the village are a few holiday parks, static caravans offering quiet locations for countryside holidays. The spot where the picture was taken is now occupied by a cottage known as The Oaks, erected in 1966.

BEITH

BEITH IS AN historical community built along an ancient main street that retains much of its old appearance – apart from one section where rather keen town planners ripped out the heart to make a short ring road. Thus, The Cross has been opened up, the old Main Street and Eglinton Street being separated on either side. The village was long famed for cotton spinning and weaving, and latterly for furniture manufacture. It also had quite a reputation for smuggling, goods being brought via the village from the coast towards Glasgow. At one time there were three distilleries in the parish. This picture shows the old Beith Academy of 1840, closed in 1999 and demolished in 2002. Next to it is the High Church, erected in 1807-10 to replace the Auld

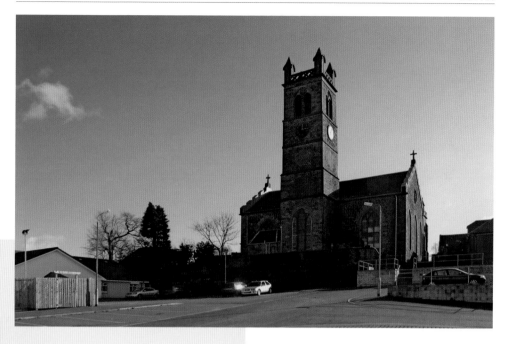

Kirk, the sixteenth-century remains of which survive in the old kirkyard at The Cross.

THE PARISH CHURCH survives, perched on Knockbuckle hill. Its 92ft-tall tower is a local landmark, earning the church the epithet the 'Visible Kirk'. The old Academy building has been demolished, the site occupied by Taigh Mor (a respite care home for people with a learning disability), and Academy Brae flats. One block has been erected on the spot where the photographer stood for the old picture. The traditional industries of furniture manufacture and tanning have gone, and today many of the residents travel for work. On the periphery of the town are large whisky bonds and defence munitions, the main employers. The centre of the village has undergone a partial facelift, the area around The Cross, and the ruins of the Old Kirk, being renovated. Included in this was the former home of Revd John Witherspoon, who was to sign the American Declaration of Independence.

CATRINE

THE VILLAGE OF Catrine was established as a new community in 1787 by the local landowner, Claud Alexander of Ballochmyle, who invited David Dale of New Lanark to assist him in building up a milling village. The River Ayr was dammed, the water passing through 'voes', seen in the foreground, before driving a huge water mill, capable of producing 200hp. At one time tourists came to Catrine just to see the wheel, one of the largest in the country. Mill buildings were constructed in the centre of the new community, producing cotton which was exported all over the country. The mill owners encouraged the workers to buy their own houses, hence the more random buildings in the village, such as St Cuthbert's Street (seen here). It was named after the ancient St Cuthbert's Chapel which stood nearby. A church was erected on the hillside in 1792 and a village institute in 1898.

THE MILLS HAVE now gone and the sites of both the old and new mills are currently open spaces in the centre of the village. The Old Mill is now the village square and the New Mill of 1950 was demolished within forty years, leaving an open area of grassland. St Cuthbert's Street has hardly changed, the voes now forming a local nature reserve, the trees and bushes growing considerably and blocking some of the more open views. The old bleaching works have been converted into a large whisky bond and bottling plant, the largest employer today. At the south-eastern side of the old part of the village the housing estate of Shawwood was erected in the 1950s and 1960s, housing miners from elsewhere in the district. Of the old buildings surviving, Nether Catrine House exists, the place where Robert Burns 'dinner'd wi' a lord' – it was the home of Professor Dugald Stewart.

COLMONELL

A SMALL SOUTH-Ayrshire village,
Colmonell sits in the middle of a large rural
parish. This view shows the Main Street
looking south-westwards towards the
prominent hill of Knockdolian. At 869ft,
it is the highest summit in the immediate
locality. Unfortunately, its prominence and
shape has caused difficulties for sailors in
the mist, for it resembles the islet of Ailsa
Craig, with dire consequences. On the left of
the picture is the Boar's Head Hotel, one of
two old inns in Colmonell at that time – the
other was the Queen's Hotel. The shop on
the right was a local store selling Melrose's
Tea and other provisions. A couple of other
small shops are located further along the
street. At the end of the street, hidden from
view, is the old parish church of 1772,
remodelled over the years.

THE BOAR'S HEAD Inn still serves the locals in the village, but the old shop has been converted into a dwelling-house, its windows remodelled and widened. Only the flutes on top of the two downpipes remain unchanged. Beyond it, most of the row of houses has been demolished, leaving a wide gap. Within this, though not obvious in the modern picture, is a small static caravan site. The Queen's Hotel is closed, but the local village hall is still in use, serving as a post office one day per week. The hall dates from 1890, but the clock tower was added to mark Queen Victoria's Diamond Jubilee in 1897. A new primary school was erected in January 2011. The village lies in attractive countryside, surrounded by three ancient castle ruins: Knockdolian, Craigneil and Kirkhill, the latter almost within the village.

CUMNOCK

CUMNOCK IS AN old community that was created a burgh of barony in 1509. It was established around the ancient Cumnock Kirk, which stood for many years before that. This old picture looks from the Lugar Bridge into the town centre, with the present 'old church' of 1866 standing in the Square. The predecessor to this church was one of 1754, designed by Robert Adam, who was working on the nearby Dumfries House. Lugar Street links the bridge, originally erected in 1753, with the Square, where the old market cross of 1703 is located. On the right is the former Jeannie House, at one time a woollen mill, and beyond is the post office building of 1911. On the left, behind the railings, stands Riverside, a coalmaster's house. The building with the pedimented windows was the Tup Inn, an old hostelry in the town, behind which is the tall Clydesdale Bank.

THE JEANNIE HOUSE was demolished in 1966 to allow the widening of the Tanyard, the street to the right, as were the low cottages. This allows a view of the Baird Institute Museum, erected in 1891 and containing many local artefacts, including an old Covenanting flag. Here also can be seen many belongings of James Keir Hardie, one of the first Labour party Members of Parliament, who lived in the town. To the left, other old houses were removed to create a new road towards Edinburgh. The Tup Inn was demolished and its site awaits redevelopment, but the Clydesdale Bank of 1883 survives, as does the post office. Today Cumnock has grown considerably, its population swollen by the demolition of a number of surrounding mining communities. The deep-mining industry has gone, replaced by opencast mining, but this does not employ as many people.

DALMELLINGTON

THERE HAS BEEN a community at
Dalmellington for centuries. In the centre
of the village is the old Norman motte
hill, and the remnants of Dame Helen's
Castle, reputedly the founder of the
village, stand nearby. In the seventeenth
century the village was noted for its
Covenanters. In the nineteenth century
the countryside around was discovered to
be plentiful in ironstone, limestone and
coal, making it an ideal spot to establish
an ironworks and associated industry.
With the arrival of the railway in 1856
trade burgeoned, and the Doon valley
communities thrived. Dalmellington
became the principal town in the area,
serving a number of outlying mining
villages. The parish church, seen at the
top of the hill known as Knowehead,

dates from 1846, replacing the old church of 1766, seen on the right of the image, itself a successor to the ancient kirk that formerly stood in the old kirkyard.

THE STREET AT Knowehead has hardly changed over the years. The 'Kirk o' the Covenant', as it is known locally, still stands, its red door reputedly that colour to represent the blood shed by the martyrs. The older church building is now the church hall. The ironworks have gone, and today the coal produced in the parish is by opencast means, resulting in much of the countryside being disfigured. Nevertheless, the community has been re-establishing itself as a place to visit, on the edge of the Galloway Hills, with a heritage museum at Cathcartston, an industrial railway museum, and on Craigengillan estate pathways have been created towards Loch Doon. For a time the village promoted itself as Scotland's 'Book Town', but lost out to Wigtown. Forestry is a major player around the village, with the Kyle Forest and Carrick Forest reaching down to the community.

DALRY

DALRY IS AN old community built on a
low hill above the confluence of the Rye
Water with the River Garnock. Courthill
Street recalls the ancient moot hill that
stood here, and the parish church in the
kirkyard occupies an ancient site. The village
was at one time home to silk weavers, who
were superseded by cotton weavers in the
eighteenth century. Later on a large mill
was built, employing hundreds of weavers.
Coal-mining was also to be a major employer
locally, with numerous pits established
around the village. The Blair ironworks
was constructed in 1839, but it was not as
successful as other Ayrshire ironworks. The
village grew considerably, however. This
view shows New Street, looking towards
the centre of the town, the White Hart Inn
in the distance. The horse and cart stand
outside the Brick House, an old inn.

THE LAST COAL mine in the parish closed in 1969, as have the spinning mills and other traditional industries. Today the main employer in the town is the Roche chemical works, a massive factory built on the north side of the community to produce Vitamin C, becoming the largest producer in the world. The population increased to almost 6,600, but has started to fall again. New Street remains much the same, the White Hart Inn, now known as the Royal Hotel, still standing at the junction with Garnock Street. A number of buildings on the right have been demolished to allow the erection of a new police station with associated parking, itself now closed. At the corner of Smith Street is a small grocery, the building dating from 1865. Both it and the former Brick House have lost their tall chimneys, located centrally on the façade.

DALRYMPLE

A SMALL VILLAGE at a crossing of the
River Doon, Dalrymple was established
around 1800 when the Marquis of Ailsa
laid out two streets: Main Street, seen
here, and Garden Street. Previously there
had only been a few cottages, 'huddled
together round the churchyard'. The
church dates from 1854, centre of an
elongated parish. However, reference
to it being annexed to the Chapel Royal
at Stirling in 1501 is known. In the
village are few commercial premises. The
Kirkton Inn stands at the junction of
the main roads, originally known as the
Dalrymple Inn. The building behind the
tree was at one time thatched and was
occupied by a small shop. Further along
the street to the right was the smiddy,
dating from 1868. On the postcard
reproduced here, Lizzie Fleming wrote,
'Do you know this girl [to the left?] This is
me and one of my school companions...'

THE OLD HOUSES on the sides of the streets remain much the same, brightly painted with the window and door surrounds picked out in different colours in the local style. The Kirkton Inn was rebuilt in the early twentieth century, its red roof and canopy being distinctive. It still serves food and ales. The village hall next door was built around 1870 with funds presented by James Stephen, a Glasgow iron-founder, who lived at Skeldon House. In the far distance is the former village smiddy. The village has grown slowly over the years, initially when miners from rows higher up the parish were rehoused here, and more recently by commuters who travel to nearby Ayr or beyond for work.

31

DARVEL

THE SMALL TOWN of Darvel can trace its establishment back to 1752 when the Earls of Loudoun granted feus for twelve houses alongside the road from Kilmarnock to Edinburgh. The community developed slowly, initially dependent on weaving, but with the arrival of the lace industry in 1876 it grew more quickly, with numerous factories producing fine lace and other goods. This view shows Hastings Square, with the tall war memorial in its centre, complete with 112 names of those killed in the First World War. A further thirty-one names were added after the Second World War. Around the Square are many nineteenth-century buildings, plus the Town Hall of 1905, parish church of 1888, and the Black Bull Inn of 1840. The shop at the corner was Walker & Connell's

stationery and printers, with West Main Street continuing into the distance. (*Courtesy of the Burns Monument Centre*)

THE PRINT WORKS of Walker and Connell (the shop at the corner was erected in 1860) only closed in recent years, but the general view remains much the same. In 1960 a memorial garden was laid out in the Square to commemorate Sir Alexander Fleming, discoverer of penicillin, who was born at Lochfield farm, just outside Darvel. It has a bronze bust of Fleming carved by E.R. Bevan. Also in the Square can be seen the Dagon Stone, an ancient standing stone relocated here, which has many local traditions associated with it. There is also a memorial to the Armed Forces that were stationed in the district during the Second World War. Erected in 2005, this lists British and Canadian regiments, including the SAS. Some lace-making still takes place in the town, but most of the large factories have been closed and demolished.

DUNDONALD

THIS EARLY VIEW shows the southern end of Dundonald's Main Street, taken from just outside the parish church. On the right is the Dundonald Inn, with a horse and cart standing outside it. At the time it was owned by Pollock and offered stabling and hiring. The single-storey buildings with the first-floor gablets are quite typical of small Ayrshire communities of the time. Farther down the street, with the dormer windows, is the Old Castle Inn. On the left, the porch belongs to the Montgomerie Hall, built in the nineteenth century as the village school. The trees mark the entrance to the manse garden. Dundonald was established in the lea of Dundonald Castle, erected on a prominent hill in the thirteenth century, but rebuilt in the 1370s by King Robert II. Boswell and Johnson paid a visit in 1773.

THIS PART OF Dundonald is now a conservation area, the traditional style of the old weavers' cottages being protected. The Montgomerie Hall is now a community hall. At the time of writing the Dundonald Inn, or 'tap pub' as the locals knew it, is closed. The 'bottom pub', or Castle Inn, survives. In the gap, at one time, were the village gas works, producing town gas for lighting. The village has been extended considerably, many houses being erected on the former Auchans estate, the mansion of which has been demolished. Dundonald Castle has been stabilised and is now open to the public, a visitor centre located half way up the hill. The parish church of 1803 survives, but the Free Church of 1843 is now its hall. Its first minister was Revd Thomas Burns, nephew of Robert Burns.

DUNLOP

THIS PART OF Dunlop was originally known as
Laighmuir and was a separate part of the village,
which was originally centred on the western half
of Main Street. The name Laighmuir has now
been superseded by Main Street, seen here at the
junction with Stewarton Road, striking to the
right, and Lugton Road, which takes a turn to
the left beyond the building with the sign. Behind
the railings on the left was the Free Church
of 1845. Hiding it is Mrs Bull's sweetie shop.
In front of the church gate can be seen an old
cast-iron water pump. On the right was Taylor's
boot and shoe shop. Dunlop is a village of some
character; old cottages line the Main Street
down to the church of 1835, adjoining an old
tomb of the seventeenth century and the former
Clandeboye School of 1641.

THE FREE CHURCH became known as the High Church latterly, and is now the parish church hall. The sweetie shop has been converted into flats, and the former shoe shop has been incorporated into the rest of the house. Dunlop is an attractive small village, the traditional houses in Main Street being typical of eighteenth-century rural village properties. At one time there was a sizeable mill here, spinning yarn for Kilmarnock carpet makers, but this has closed. Among the interesting buildings are Kirkland, the former manse of the sixteenth century, rebuilt in 1910, and the village hall of 1891. In the kirkyard is the grave of Barbara Gilmour, inventor of Dunlop cheese. The village population is a little more than 800, having risen slowly over the years.

DUNURE

THE FISHING VILLAGE of Dunure lies at the foot of the Carrick Hills. There is a small square harbour, squeezed between the rocks, its tiny light beacon notable for the eroded stones from which it was built. The harbour was originally constructed for exporting coal, but this died off quickly and it was then used for fishing boats. In the foreground of this postcard, taken from the castle battlements, is the beehive doocot, dating from the sixteenth century, which still has its stone nesting boxes within. To the right of the doocot is an eighteenth-century two-draw limekiln.

THE ANCIENT DOOCOT still stands, as does the limekiln. A few more houses have been built on the hillside, but the double-storey block in the old village has gone. Today Dunure is a small commuter village, one that attracts tourists to its quaint harbour, where small fishing vessels and pleasure craft tie up. The castle ruins have been stabilised, and visitors can view the ruins more readily, imagining the time when the commendator of Crossraguel Abbey was roasted over a fire in the Black Vault to persuade him to hand over the abbey lands to the Kennedy laird.

FAIRLIE

THE ANCIENT COMMUNITY at Fairlie comprised of three rows of houses, one mainly occupied by weavers (the South Row), by fishermen (the Middle Row, next to the sea and a small harbour), and by craftsmen (the North Row). Like Largs and Skelmorlie, the village grew with the erection of large villas, used for holidays. One of the houses, Creich, was built for Hugh Tennent, who introduced lager to Scotland, creating Tennent's brewery in Glasgow. A church was erected in 1834, and Fife's boatyard made exceptional yachts for many years, including craft made for the kings of Denmark and Spain, and Sir William Lipton. On the hillside above the village stands Fairlie Castle, at one time the seat of the Fairlie's of that ilk. This view shows Main Road, at the north end of the village. On the left is the Kelburn Arms Hotel, dating from the 1880s.

TODAY FAIRLIE HAS few businesses in the village, even although there are more residents than when the older image was taken. The Kelburn Arms has been demolished, and the garage is closed, its main shed a rusting hulk. The little Evergreen Cottage survives, with the larger sandstone buildings adjoining it. Next again are modern flats, and in the contemporary view the parish church is visible, with its spire. On the right, beyond the house with the two dormer windows, known as The Neuk, are a row of shops, occupied by a florist, Chinese carry-out, sandwich shop and a plumber's office. The buildings beyond have been demolished, the land used for parking. Fife's boatyard has been cleared away, the site used for housing. In the gap in the wall on the right is a memorial to Queen Victoria, originally a fountain, opened on the day Edward VII was crowned.

GALSTON

CLAIMING TO BE the 'Heart' of Ayrshire, Galston is an old community that was built around its castle. The foursquare tower of Barr Castle can be seen to the left of the image, a building that dates from the fifteenth century. To the left again can be seen the parish church, with spire, erected in 1808. In the kirkyard are Covenanter graves, as well as that of Revd Robert Stirling, who invented the Stirling engine. St Sophia's church is in the centre of the picture, a rather strange brick-built chapel based on the Hagia Sophia in Istanbul. In the distance can be seen the large Loudoun Castle, said to be the 'Windsor of the North'. In the middle foreground are the old rows of Howie's Square, built for local mineworkers. The picture was taken from the hill south of the town at Burnhousehill.

THE CEMETERY HAS been extended over the years, but much of the view remains the same.
Loudoun Castle, however, was burned out in 1941 and remains a ruinous shell. From 1996 it was
the centre of a theme park, now closed. In the parkland the Loudoun Gowf (the old Scots word
for golf) Club was established in 1909. There are no coal mines in the parish now, and the miners'
rows of Howie's Square have been replaced by the bungalows of Carnalea Court. The two churches
survive, and Barr Castle is now home to a masonic temple, with a museum of local artefacts on the
top floor. The two chimneys seen in the old picture have gone – these belonged to lace mills which
closed in the 1960s. The large building above the castle is Loudoun Academy, the local secondary
school, opened in 1969.

GIRVAN

AN IMPORTANT FISHING port, Girvan stands at the mouth of the river of that name. It was established as a burgh in 1668. The harbour is formed in the estuary, and at one time steamers called here on their tours of the Firth of Clyde. The sandy beach has always been popular with holidaymakers, and Girvan grew with the arrival of the railway, making it more accessible for city-dwellers to take to the country. As a result, new terraces of large villas were added around the old town. Also famed for its early potatoes, the local farmers still grow these along the sandy foreshore. This view shows Dalrymple Street looking north, past the junction of Ailsa Street. Crosbie's ironmongery was established in 1826. Behind it is the corner tower of the MacKechnie Institute, built in 1888 and housing a small museum.

PERHAPS THE ONLY building still operating much as it did is the MacKechnie Institute, home to exhibitions, museum items and meeting rooms. The roadway has been reduced in width, forming a one-way route, to allow wider pavements. This was done to improve facilities for visitors, trying to promote the town as a holiday destination at a time when most people holiday abroad. Yet Girvan still attracts tourists on a shorter break – there are numerous hotels and caravan sites in the locality, and the beach is still popular with children. The harbour remains a popular spot to visit, fishing boats and pleasure yachts sharing the berths. Noble's boatyard, established in 1946, builds and repairs fishing vessels. Most of the shops have changed hands, but Crosbie's building is still an ironmongery. The building on the right with the post office is built on the site of a church.

IRVINE

ONE OF AYRSHIRE'S larger towns, Irvine is an ancient burgh, located at the mouth of the river of the same name. Created a royal burgh in 1372, in 1966 it became one of Scotland's new towns. This view shows High Street, with the tall tower of the Town House. This was erected in 1859, to the plans of Ayrshire architect, James Ingram. At one time the market cross stood in front, its site marked by a ring of cobbles. Across the road can be made out the pedestal on

which stands the statue of David Boyle, Lord Shewalton, noted in history as the man who sentenced Burke (of Burke and Hare infamy) to death. The street is lined with Scots vernacular buildings, such as the ironmongery store on the left, followed by J. Mitchell's. The last shop before the Town House was Thomas Scott's wines and spirits shop.

THE BLACK MAN, as Boyle's statue was known, was moved from the street to help traffic flow in 1929. Between the eras of the two pictures, the war memorial, based on the design of a traditional market cross, has come and gone from the centre of the street. Scott's shop survives as one of the few old buildings remaining in the High Street – though it now sells fish and chips. The New Town did much to destroy the heart of old Irvine, many buildings being cleared away in the name of progress. The old buildings in the old photograph were replaced before the time of the New Town, the ironmongery store by a branch of Irvine and Fullarton Co-operative, now Iceland supermarket, and Mitchell's by a utilitarian co-operative shop. Beyond the Town House the tall buildings have been demolished – Henry Eckford, a co-founder of the American navy, may have lived there.

47

KILBIRNIE

THE WILLIAM KNOX Institute stands at the north end of Main Street, the building erected in 1892 for the benefit of the people of Kilbirnie. The donor was the Knox family, who owned the large spinning mills for which Kilbirnie was at one time noted. To the left of the institute can be seen the tall three-storey Stoneyholm Mills building, with simple pediment and tall chimney behind. Originally a cotton mill, it was later a fishing-net factory. Between the mill and the institute flows the River Garnock, with Garnock Bridge crossing it, and Garnock Street behind. The rest of the town is a long-straggling community, the ancient parish church rather remotely located at the southern end. This dates from 1470, with a tower of around 1490. Many houses were added when the Glengarnock steel works was established in the mid-nineteenth century.

THE STEELWORKS AT Glengarnock have gone, closed in 1979, and most mill buildings in the town have closed down. The Stoneyholm Mills buildings are closed and currently stand forlorn, but W. & J. Knox, founded in 1778, still make large fishing nets in a new factory located behind them. The houses in Garnock Street have been razed, the site of them for a time replaced by a rather indistinct police station, itself demolished in recent years. Today the site is occupied by a supermarket car park. The Knox Institute has been shorn of its corner spirelet, but the building survives, dominating a roundabout at the junction of Main Street with Bridgend. The old bridge has been widened to create a roundabout. Kilbirnie has a population of around 7,000 today, a figure that has declined from its peak of over 8,000.

KILMARNOCK

THE SECOND TOWN of Ayrshire, Kilmarnock was the county's industrial centre. Here were major factories producing carpets, valves, sanitary items, whisky, shoes, railway engines, tractors, and many other examples of good workmanship. At one time the population was in excess of Ayr, the thriving community having a busy shopping centre, seen here in this view of The Cross, looking down King Street from Portland Street. The baronial building on the left stood at the end of Duke Street. On the other side of Duke Street was Lewis's department store. The spire behind it belonged to Kilmarnock Town Hall, built in 1805. Next again is the prominent National Bank building. On the right was David Lauder's Ironmongers (upstairs), established

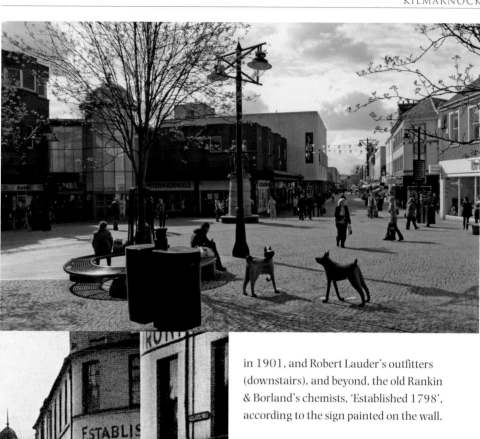

in 1901, and Robert Lauder's outfitters (downstairs), and beyond, the old Rankin & Borland's chemists, 'Established 1798', according to the sign painted on the wall.

ALMOST ALL OF the major industries have now gone from the town: even the famous Johnnie Walker whisky is no longer being blended and bottled here, the factory closing in 2012. The Cross has changed too: it is now pedestrianized. The Town Hall was demolished, along with Lewis's and the baronial building, to create a modern, but bland, shopping centre. Duke Street exists no more – built over with an indoor shopping centre and new ring road. King Street has been pedestrianized, but it still struggles to compete with out-of-town supermarkets and shopping centres in Glasgow. In fact, virtually every building in the old image has been demolished, apart from that in the distance with the domed turret. In the centre of The Cross is a double statue of Robert Burns and his printer, John Wilson, for Burns' first 'Kilmarnock' edition was printed nearby.

KILMAURS

THIS IS A very early view of the Toonheid of Kilmaurs, looking north from near the Wheatsheaf
Inn. The proper name of the street historically was Main Street, but to locals it has always been the
Toonheid. In the foreground is a water pump, the iron work typical of that made in Kilmarnock
by Glenfield & Kennedy. Away at the top of the hill was a toll cottage, in the gusset of Stewarton
Road and Standalane. Across from the light-coloured gable end was the village smiddy. Kilmaurs is
an old parish centre, and there are many traditional buildings surviving at the village heart. Most
important of these is the old Town House or tollbooth – better known locally as 'The Jougs', after

the iron neck-ring used to lock up malefactors. This dates from the seventeenth century, though the steeple was added later. (*Courtesy of the Burns Monument Centre*)

ALTHOUGH KILMAURS APPEARS to be an old village with many traditional buildings, virtually every house in the old image has been demolished and the site rebuilt with fairly recent council houses. As can be seen, these were built in a traditional style, blending with the rest of the village. The pump has gone, allowing the street to be widened. The building that faced down the Toonheid was removed prior to the 1930s, allowing the creation of Vine Park Avenue. The rest of the row was removed later. The old centre of Kilmaurs remains much as it always has: The Jougs still in the middle of the road, and the old weavers' cottages lining the streets. Around it is the old Public Hall of 1892, and the Weston Tavern of 1740, although at that time it was a manse. Outwith the village proper is the parish church of 1888.

KILWINNING

KILWINNING GREW UP around the ancient abbey, founded in 1188 by the Tironensian abbots. The remains of the building survive in the centre of the town, the gable visible to the right of the tall tower. This tower was erected in 1816 to replace an older tower which had collapsed two years earlier. The village grew with the establishment of the Eglinton Ironworks in 1846, which employed over 1,000 men at one time. Surrounding the town were coal mines. This view shows the Howgate, the old road to the west. The buildings on the left date from the second half of the nineteenth century – that on the immediate left becoming the burgh chambers in 1930. The building at the far end of the street, with its large sign, is the Victoria Bar. To the right, the gateway behind the stone wall led into the manse.

THE IRONWORKS WAS closed in 1924 and the community declined for some time thereafter. In 1966 Kilwinning was included within Irvine New Town, resulting in much new development. A number of large factories were established, and new housing estates added around the core, such as Pennyburn and Whitehirst Park. Unfortunately, much of the new industry didn't last long, but the town survives, home now to a branch of James Watt College. The abbey tower is now a visitor attraction, allowing folk to climb to the top. Here also the ancient sport of papingo shooting takes place, the Kilwinning Archers being one of the longest-surviving groups in the world. Much of the view remains the same, but some of the buildings in the middle of the row to the left were demolished to allow the creation of Lauchlan Way, a short ring road around Main Street, which was subsequently pedestrianized.

LARGS

FOR MANY YEARS Largs has been a coastal resort frequented by holidaymakers leaving the urban sprawl of Glasgow and Paisley behind to enjoy a day, or longer, at the seaside. The town, however, has a longer history, mentioned as early as the Battle of Largs in 1263, when the Scots finally defeated Viking control of the west of the country – a monument to the victory stands by the shore. The centre of a parish of its own, Largs was for many years a market community, and this view shows Main Street. In the early 1800s a well was located in the centre of the street. At the far end was the Tron Tree, or market weigh-place. Taken in the early 1900s, this view depicts Peter Bonini's confectionary shop on the right, and Peter Watson's grocery at the corner of Greenock Road, typical of the town, serving locals and visitors alike.

THE TOWN IS still a very popular destination for day-trippers, and numerous shops cater to their needs – from gift shops to confectioners, fish and chip shops to clothes shops. Main Street is still the main thoroughfare, the corner shop now the Clydesdale Bank. The building with the tall adorned gable is the Royal Bank, dating from 1900. The right-hand side of the street has been rebuilt as far ás Bath Street. Nardini's ice-cream parlour is located within the modern Moorings building, which dates from 1990, replacing an older, art deco Moorings of 1936, itself built on the site of Bonini's shop. The famous Nardini café is located overlooking the Esplanade, but it is no longer owned by the family. Beyond Bath Street the business premises occupy buildings that have also been rebuilt since the old image, dating from between the wars.

LENDALFOOT

A TINY CLACHAN on the shores of the Firth of Clyde, Lendalfoot lies at the mouth of the Lendal Water. It was only really a stopping-off point for travellers heading between Ayr and Stranraer, though at one time it had a busy trade in fishing. Carleton Fishery lies at the far end of the bay, boats originally having to be hauled on to the shingle shore. This postcard view was taken from the Deafstone, a large natural rock in the field, left on the geological raised beach when the land rose out of the water. In the foreground is the village smiddy. The double-storey building with the smoke was the village school. The steep slopes of Balsalloch

Hill rise behind. In 1937 there were plans to create a new holiday resort along the foot of it, but the plans didn't materialise.

THE OLD SMIDDY is now a cottage, and fishing is no longer carried on from the fishery. Today the village is home to many holiday homes and caravans. Many small huts and lodges have been built along the shore at the foot of Balsalloch Hill, occupied by holidaymakers who love the wild shores and hills of Carrick. The old school was converted into an outdoor centre. Near to the village are two memorials to shipwrecks: one at the north end of the village from 1711, when a ship under Captain Hamilton from King's Cross on Arran sank; the other to the south, commemorating the *Varyag*, an important Russian cruiser that sank here in 1920. The latter memorial was unveiled in 2007, a sizeable bronze cross funded from Russia. The remains of the ship still lie in the waters off the shore.

59

THE MAIDENS

THE VILLAGE KNOWN today as 'The Maidens' was originally called Douglaston. In the mid-nineteenth century it was little more than a few houses along the shore, such as Wearyneuk (supposedly named by Robert the Bruce), Seafield, Clachanton and Sandhouse. There was also a small chemical works, which became the cottages in the middle of the picture. By the turn of the twentieth century, the Maidenhead Rocks had been linked to the mainland by a short pier, creating a harbour suitable for fishing boats. There was even a small shipbuilding yard located in the village. A small community built up in the area, the white building being the school. A small chapel of ease was also erected, services being held in the summer, gaining it the moniker the 'Holidaymakers' church'. In the foreground is Norway Cottage, and behind it Wearyneuk Block, built to house workers.

TODAY THE VILLAGE is a popular holiday resort, there probably being more caravans in the community than houses. A considerable number of houses have also been added to the village, creating a more compact community. A number of hotels have been established, and the beach continues to be an attraction for children. The old school is now the community centre, a new school erected elsewhere. The harbour is no longer a fishing port, but in 2011 new pontoons for pleasure craft were created, attracting yachts to the harbour. The harbour was liable to silting, and the present image shows how much land has been reclaimed as a result. Part of the ground was utilised by Maidens Bowling Club, the green surrounded by the red fence. The Wearyneuk Block has gone, replaced by the Bruce Hotel, which was later renamed Wildings.

MAUCHLINE

THE CROSS IS the centre of Mauchline, where the main roads meet. It was not always so, for Earl Grey Street in the distance was only created around 1820, replacing the old but narrow Cowgate as the main route south. On the left is Mauchline Place, a large townhouse of the Gibbs, built in 1756. Latterly it was divided into flats but it became a 'disgrace' to the village. Beyond, the building with the arched pend, is the Black Bull Inn. The printing works on the right were owned by J. Dickie, who produced the *Mauchline & Catrine News and Advertiser* for a short time in 1908. The building has a local tradition connecting it with the execution of five Covenanters buried at the Loan Green in 1685. At the time it was Mr Fisher's Inn. Mr Fisher supplied the executioner with rope, and thereafter the locals claimed that the building was cursed.

THE BASIC LAYOUT of The Cross remains unchanged. The old printing works have been rebuilt and are currently occupied by a dental surgery. An old date stone of 1748 survives. Mauchline Place was demolished in the 1930s, and even the post office built on its site has itself been removed, the site now occupied by a library and flats of 1996. In front of it stands a statue of Jean Armour, wife of the poet Robert Burns, who lived in the village for a number of years, writing some of his best works here. Many other places in the village have Burns associations, such as the Castle, Poosie Nansie's Inn and Burns' house itself. Earl Grey Street still has the bank and the Black Bull, and a few other shops. Street furniture and public realm works clutter the openness of The Cross compared to the old days.

MAYBOLE

TAKEN FROM AN old glass negative, this view shows High Street as viewed from Whitehall. At the far end stands Maybole Castle, built by the Kennedy family. Tradition claims that the gypsies came here and stole away the laird's wife, only for him to catch them later and execute them at his other castle of Cassillis. The town is an ancient one, claiming to be the 'Capital of

Carrick', and at one time there were a number of old tower houses in it, town houses for Carrick lairds. To the right, its ornate corbelling just visible, was the castle of the Kennedys of Blairquhan, later converted into a tolbooth and town hall. On the left was Henderson's stationery, MacCulloch's clockmakers and Cameron's hardware emporium, established in 1843. At one time the town was noted for the manufacture of 'Maybole' boots and shoes, as well as agricultural implements.

MANY OF THE shops in Maybole's main thoroughfare have closed, and others are rather neglected externally. The town still retains a degree of traditional style, most of the older properties along the roadside still surviving. The town hall is still a busy venue for meetings, and the castle at the far end of the street has been acquired by the community for development as a meeting place and heritage centre. No boots or leather are made in the town today, and the agricultural implement works of Alexander Jack was recently demolished. Most of the residents now travel to Ayr or beyond for work, there being no major industries left. The town has a new church building of 2012, one of the two churches that merged to form the present congregation being converted into housing.

MUIRKIRK

THE VILLAGE OF Muirkirk was really only established in 1631 when part of Sorn parish was separated to form a new parish, with a church originally called the 'Moor Kirk of Kyle'. Little happened for many years until the eighteenth century when the area was discovered to contain useful supplies of coal, ironstone and limestone, allowing the establishment of a large ironworks in 1787. The village grew thereafter, reaching a peak population of 5,000 around 1900. John Loudoun MacAdam, the famous roadmaker, had a tar works in the village, now marked by a cairn. The old church dates from 1812 and in the kirkyard is a Covenanter's grave, as well as that of John Lapraik and Tibbie Pagan, poets. The Kames pit was one of the largest in the

locality, but in 1957 there was a disaster with the loss of seventeen lives. This old view shows Main Street, looking east, with a selection of shops and houses.

MANY OF THE buildings on the north side of the street survive, but unfortunately, with the loss of deep mining and a consequential drop in population, many of them are empty and looking forlorn. On the south side of the street various premises have been demolished, opening up the streetscape, allowing some more modern buildings to take their place. The surrounding countryside has been ravaged by opencast coal mines, but the moors still remain in many places, noted for their wildlife. The ironworks were closed in 1923, Kames Pit in 1968, and today most residents have to travel for work. Nevertheless, the village remains a vibrant community, much-loved by its residents. At the village centre, in a small open area, a statue was erected in 2004 commemorating all of the men who lost their lives in the local coal mines. At Smallburn, by the roadside, a heritage area details some more of the parish's historical connections.

NEWMILNS

NEWMILNS WAS CREATED a free burgh of
barony in 1490 by King James IV, the first
inland burgh in Ayrshire. The village grew
slowly thereafter, but in the mid-eighteenth
century linen weaving became a local industry.
This changed to cotton weaving, and soon
this was the major employer. In 1877 Joseph
Hood introduced the first power loom to the
village, and by the end of the Victorian period
there were numerous large mills producing
lace, in addition to cotton. This view of Main
Street shows the old town house, with the
open stairs to the upper floor and the bellcote
above. The building was erected in 1739, the
lower floor vaulted for cells, the upper room
being the council's chamber. In front stands the
fountain presented in 1890 by Miss Brown of
Lanfine. On the right, the large building is the
eighteenth-century Loudoun Arms Inn.

THE VIEW REMAINS much the same today. The old town house has been restored and is the office of the Irvine Valley Regeneration Partnership, which is making improvements to living conditions in the district. The partnership has restored many older properties in the village centre, improving the appearance. It has also developed a paths network in the valley and established a walking festival. The Loudoun Arms has also been renovated, and continues to satisfy the thirst of locals. Behind it is the ancient Newmilns Tower, associated with the Covenanters. The former Bridgend Bar, which is seen at the end of the road, is now a Chinese takeaway. Miss Brown's fountain has been removed. Unfortunately, most of the lace mills in the valley have gone, and with them much of the employment. Three lace and braid factories remain, however. Today, Newmilns is more of a dormitory town.

NEW
CUMNOCK

THE MAIN STREET passing through New Cumnock is known as the 'Castle' from the fact that anciently the Black Bog or Cumnock Castle stood on a low hillock here. The site is now occupied by the former Arthur Memorial Church, but no remnants of the castle remain. The village grew up around the old castle, as well as the parish church, which still stands in ruins in the kirkyard. The light-coloured building in this 1960s view is the Castle Hotel, at one time visited by Robert Burns. He has a number of associations with the village, and his 'Afton Water' is a well-known song. To the right of the hotel is Biddell's Regal Cinema, followed by a line of shops, including the National Commercial Bank of Scotland. On the left of the street were the old post office and a line of commercial premises. (*Courtesy of the Burns Monument Centre*)

THE LINE OF shops and flats on the left of the street have all been demolished, their site now occupied by local authority housing, set back from the road. Adjoining, in an open area of grass, is a granite memorial commemorating all of the local miners who lost their lives in the many coal mines for which New Cumnock was noted. These have all gone, but the village is surrounded by numerous opencast mines, still extracting coal in the parish. The population has slumped from the boom years of the 1960s, resulting in many houses being demolished – whole streets of them, in some cases. The Castle is no longer the bustling shopping area it once was, the picture house being just one of the buildings that has been removed. The Castle Hotel is now a private house, and the old coaching inn known as the Crown Hotel is closed up.

OCHILTREE

THIS PART OF Ochiltree's long Main Street was known variously as Weir's Brae or the Smiddy Brae, after the smiddy building which was located at its foot. The double-storey building to the left of the lamp post, with the boot-scraper on the step, was at one time the location of the Free Church School on the upper floor. The buildings with the sun canopies were commercial premises, and down at the foot of the street can be seen the old market cross. Behind the photographer, further up the street, is the parish church of 1769, the old school of 1908, and the 'House with the Green

Shutters', birthplace of George Douglas Brown, who wrote a novel of that name in 1901 which put an end to the Scot 'kailyard' school of writing. The book is still in print. At one time Ochiltree was noted for the manufacture of toddy ladles and sickles.

THE GENERAL APPEARANCE of the village has changed little. A few of the older thatched cottages have been demolished or else rebuilt in more permanent materials. On the horizon in the old view can be made out the Barony Colliery of 1906, replaced in the modern picture by a chipboard factory, and the preserved A-frame of the colliery. Mining is no longer a local occupation, apart from a few surface mines, and the village is really only a dormitory village, there being no industry or large employers. A few small shops survive, such as the general store and post office, with the signs lower down the hill, plus another general store, a tyre-fitter, carry-out restaurant and caterer. The church survives, but the Free Church School is a distant memory, and the present school dates from 1976. The old school building has been divided into dwellings.

PATNA

ALTHOUGH THERE WAS a tiny community at Patna in the eighteenth century, the present village owes its existence to William Fullarton of Skeldon (1775-1835), who owned the local estate of Keirs. He also had property in India and it is claimed that the Ayrshire village was named after the great city on the Ganges. The community was established in the first decade of the nineteenth century to house workers in the limestone quarries and coal pits that he established. The village soon began to grow. Being in Straiton parish, a church was added in 1837 to save parishioners from walking across the moor to worship. The church in the postcard view is the former Free Church of 1903. The memorial fountain was the gift of A. Barclay Walker of Liverpool in 1872. He was a former resident who established a brewery in Liverpool.

THE WALKER FOUNTAIN has suffered: its crown has been removed. Most of the older buildings have been demolished, including the old miners' rows, replaced by more modern council or private housing. Today Patna has little of any antiquity surviving, but a son, James MacCosh, became President of Princeton University in America. Most of the stone-built dwellings and shops on the Main Street, seen in the picture, have gone, and many more lie disused. The ironworks and mines, which employed the bulk of the population at one time, have gone, leaving residents little option but to commute to Ayr and beyond for employment. The former Free Church is also closed, its stained glass removed to the parish church. In the distance, the Green Hill of Dunaskin remains unchanged, but the dark spoil heaps of the opencast coal mines disfigure the landscape.

PINWHERRY

PINWHERRY IS ONE of many small clachans in Ayrshire that can hardly be described as a village, but which has some degree of a community about it, and a long enough history to make it more notable than most. It lies at the foot of the Duisk River, where it meets the River Stinchar. The Duisk is bridged in the community, seen at the end of the road on the left of the image, with the old toll cottage located at its northern end, with central chimney stalk. To its right, behind the trees, is the village school, serving a wider community of farms and remote cottages. The castle, seen in ruins and covered in ivy on the right of the picture, makes Pinwherry more important than many clachans. This L-planned tower probably dates from the 1590s, when it was owned by John Kennedy.

TODAY THE CASTLE still stands in ruins, its walls crumbling ever more, though most of the ivy covering has been removed. This has revealed a decaying rubble ruin, with few hints of ornate carving, other than some corbels. The old cottages have been adapted for modern living, the first one, the gatehouse to Pinwherry House, having a new porch and dormer windows, the pair of cottages behind also having porches and new rooms in the roof space. The old toll cottage has gone, its site now little more than a few tubs containing flowers. The MacGarvie public hall in the village was opened in 1914. The school building still survives, having been built in 1898, but the school was closed on Thursday, 30 June 2011, pupils transferring to a new school built in Colmonell.

PRESTWICK

FAMED TODAY FOR its airport and golf course,
Prestwick was one of Ayrshire's older burghs.
The original community was built along
the main street running north–south, with
the parish church at the north end. This old
building survives in ruins within its kirkyard,
located on a low hillock. It dates from the
twelfth century. Prestwick had many weavers
living in it at one time, and by the shore there
were salt pans, making salt from evaporating
sea water. Inland, there were some coal mines
for a time, the community of Glenburn being
established to house the miners. This view
shows Prestwick Cross, with the post office
building of the 1920s. The market cross itself
is said to be one of Scotland's oldest, and
was renovated in 1777. On the ground can
be seen the tramlines, Prestwick being the
northernmost terminus of the Ayr trams.

PRESTWICK RETAINS A rather attractive selection of independent shops, enticing shoppers who prefer individuality as opposed to the regular chain stores. The buildings around The Cross remain much the same: the post office still functions as such, with a shop within, called the Post Box, selling gifts as well as postal services. The white building next door was Bremner's grocery, followed by Cameron's grocery – it is now a hair and beauty salon. The wall around Boydfield house has been removed, opening up the gardens, and there the war memorial was erected, commemorating the sons of the burgh who made the ultimate sacrifice. This was built in 1921, to designs by local architect James Morris. The Town Hall building is located to the right, over the shops, the arched doorway and monogram 'PC' being all that identifies it externally.

SALTCOATS

DOCKHEAD STREET IS the principal shopping street in Saltcoats, seen here at the junction with Windmill Street to the right. The town is old, having been established as a burgh of barony in 1529. The name derives from the houses where the salt-workers lived, and for many years this was the principal industry. Later, the harbour was used for fishing and exporting coal to Ireland, and inland mining became a major employer. The building second from the left was the Crown Temperance Hotel, just one of many places where holidaymakers could spend a week. It has an old Cyclist's Touring Club roundel on the wall. Behind the photographer was the Holly House Temperance Hotel, and numerous other hostelries (some offering alcohol) existed along the front, overlooking the sandy bays. The town also had numerous eventide or welfare homes, offering fresh air and respite to weary workers.

THE OLD CROWN INN still survives, now just as a pub, having been established in 1765. Most of the building has been sold to other businesses, but the CTC logo is still on the wall. Dockhead Street has been pedestrianized, allowing shoppers more freedom to wander from shop to shop. The large building on the right, at the corner of Windmill Street, is the same one, though its outward appearance has changed a bit. Today it is occupied by a travel agent and hairdresser. The building next door is a modern replacement with glass windows on the upper floors. On the left, at the junction of Chapelwell Street, is a modern building occupied by Ladbrokes and the TSB bank, with clock spirelet, erected in 1986. The old parish church has been converted into North Ayrshire Museum, holding a fascinating collection of local memorabilia and records.

SKELMORLIE

THE MOST NORTHERLY village in Ayrshire, Skelmorlie was not established until the mid-1800s, when the landowners feued their property. The village is divided into two halves: Upper Skelmorlie, which was built above the cliff-line, and Lower Skelmorlie, where this view was taken, built in a straggling line along the road, between the shore and the cliff. By 1855 there were only a few cottages along the shore road, plus the church, erected in 1856. The Beach House was the largest villa in the village, built in 1844 for the son of a Lord Provost of Edinburgh. By the later Victorian period the village had grown considerably, with numerous large villas built, in many cases for Glasgow businessmen who wanted out of the polluted city, if only for the weekend or holidays. The large Skelmorlie Hydropathic hotel was built in 1868, and others followed.

THE POSTCARD VIEW shows how Shore Road looked around 1900, with horses and carts the only transport in the street. Today, the same view has a constant stream of cars making their way along the Ayrshire coastline. On the left, the two shops are now occupied by a Chinese restaurant, the building dating from 1856. The next block is of a similar date, and now has the post office and newsagent in the middle building – originally there were five commercial premises in this terrace. The farthest shop used to be the Clydesdale Bank, now converted into Bank House. Beyond are Waters Edge flats. Skelmorlie Hydro has gone, closed in 1984 and demolished three years later, but Upper Skelmorlie still has numerous other large houses, many divided into flats.

SORN

THE ORIGINAL VILLAGE established on this site was known as Dalgain, after the local estate. A planned village of the mid-1700s, it had a single long main street, originally known as Dalgain Street. Ownership of the estate passed to Sorn Castle, and within a short time the village adopted that name. On the left can be seen the former Greyhound Inn, still thatched, which was established in 1782, and next to it the Constitutional Hall, operated by a club established in 1832. At one end of the village is the old parish kirk of 1658, located in its graveyard. Opposite it Sorn Old Bridge crosses the River Ayr, quaintly located by the old mill. Along the street shown here were a few small shops and businesses, including the usual premises in small villages – grocer's, baker's, post office, shoemaker's, drapers', joined by a branch of Catrine Co-operative in 1926.

STILL AN ATTRACTIVE small village, a fair number of the older buildings lining the main road were demolished and replaced with newer houses and cottages, often located back from the street-line with front gardens. This has created a more open streetscape. The Greyhound Inn itself was closed in 1991 and converted into homes. In the picture can be seen Sorn Primary School, the original building dating from 1849, with room for 216 pupils. In 2012 it was extended and restored, the clock tower getting a new spirelet surmounting it. The double-storey building on the right has been demolished, replaced by a garage and modern bungalow. Today Sorn has fewer commercial premises, other than the general store and post office. The Sorn Inn is the only public house in the village, but there is a popular bowling green of 1977 and village hall of 1954.

STEVENSTON

STEVENSTON IS AN old community, centre of its own parish. The town is rather straggling, with part of it located at the north end of New Street, where Main Street and Townhead Street forms the old nucleus. Here, on a prominent location, stands the parish church of 1832, its site much older. More modern housing spreads north from here. At the southern end of New Street one heads towards Ardeer, something of a suburb, extended considerably when Alfred Nobel built his explosives works here in 1873. The town had extensive coal works for many years, and quarrying was carried out for a time at Ardeer. This picture shows Moorpark Road West, which leads from New Street. The building on the left was the institute. At the end of the road on the right were St John's Roman Catholic Chapel and School. Further on were Auchenharvie Cottages, occupied by miners.

THE CHAPEL AND school building have gone, though the schoolhouse still remains, surrounded by modern housing, forming Westpark Court. The remaining houses are virtually unchanged. The old institute has been converted into a place of worship for the Jehovah's Witnesses. In the foreground, the roadway gives access to Caley Court, a sheltered housing complex. Stevenston has lost the large ICI factory, and no major employer has come in to take its place, despite the creation of the Stevenston and Nobel industrial estates. The long New Street has lost much of its importance as a commercial centre, edge of town supermarkets and retail outlets drawing the customers elsewhere. Coal-mining has long-gone, as has the quarrying industry, both leaving behind holes in the ground that are often water-filled, now surrounded by Ardeer and Auchenharvie parks.

STEWARTON

KNOWN AS THE 'Bonnet Town' from its historical industry of bonnet making, Stewarton is an attractive community located within its own parish. This old postcard view depicts Avenue Square, with the Institute Hall at the top end of the open space. The Institute Hall was erected in the late eighteenth century. This was originally the Cuninghame Institute, and for a time was Stewarton Academy. The road continues to the left as Avenue Street, the photographer standing looking up from Main Street. Avenue Street was created by the Cuninghames as a formal approach to their Corsehill property, but it was never completed. Not visible, but to its right, is the Town House – the town became a police burgh in 1868. At one time the parish war memorial was located in this

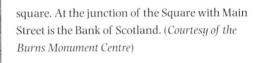

square. At the junction of the Square with Main Street is the Bank of Scotland. (*Courtesy of the Burns Monument Centre*)

STEWARTON HISTORICAL SOCIETY runs a small museum within the Town House, depicting aspects of the town's history. Stewarton is noted as being the birthplace of David Dale, creator of New Lanark mills on the Clyde, although his exact birthplace cannot be determined. Today Stewarton is a growing community, popular with commuters who travel to Glasgow or Kilmarnock for work, the population in excess of 6,500. In the contemporary view the bank remains, the old buildings across the street still having small businesses in them, such as Annick Art shop, a hairdresser's and shoe repair shop. The Institute Hall is being developed at the time of writing. Still in existence is one bonnet factory, Robert Mackie of Scotland, established in 1845. They make traditional Scottish bonnets, hats and gloves, as well as Glengarries and Balmorals for the Armed Forces.

STRAITON

AN ATTRACTIVE VILLAGE, Straiton lies in the valley of the Water of Girvan, near where it leaves its hilly hinterland to enter more lowland countryside. Originally the village comprised of a single street, but a few roads have been added since. It was established as a new community by Thomas, Earl of Cassillis, around 1760. The old parish church dates from 1758, but to its rear is an older transept of around 1510, in which is located the burial vault of the Kennedys of Blairquhan Castle. On the right of the picture is the old Black Bull Inn, the building of which dates from 28 June 1766. The village post office and shop stands on

the other side of the street, in a building with two dormer windows. The post office was later to move into the old school building. At the far end of the street stands the war memorial.

THE MAIN STREET remains much the same as it was, the old cottages lovingly cared for by their owners. What was the post office is now The Buck, offering coffees and cakes to visitors. The post office opens for a few hours per week, in a tiny shop operated by Straiton Village Co-operative. The Black Bull is still open for business, and behind the photographer is the MacCandlish Hall of 1912. The village promotes itself as being in 'rambler country' and a number of local walks can be made alongside the Water of Girvan and its tributaries, as well as to the summits of some local hills, especially Highgate Hill, on which stands a massive obelisk commemorating Colonel James Hunter Blair, who was killed at Inkerman, during the Crimean wars. He was from the nearby castle of Blairquhan, a magnificent Tudoresque mansion erected in 1820.

TROON

THE ANCIENT NAME for Troon was 'Truwyn', which was an approximation of the Gaelic *An t-Sron*, meaning the nose. This refers to its position on a headland, jutting into Ayr Bay. There was probably a small fishing clachan here for many years, but in 1808 the Duke of Portland, who owned much of the land hereabouts, decided to establish a port here. This was quite successful, and soon a fair-sized town appeared, the streets laid out on a variation of the grid system, with wide terraces and crescents following the natural layout of the land. The town became known for its golf links, Royal Troon being one of the main courses used in the Open tournament. Large villas and holiday homes were built by Glasgow businessmen, giving the town a prosperous appearance. This view shows Ayr Street, with the parish church spire of 1837 on the left.

LITTLE HAS CHANGED in this current view, though note that the oriel window on the façade of the Royal Bank of Scotland (erected in 1900) has been removed. The line of shops, built from red Mauchline sandstone, remains, offering a variety of independent retailers, for which Troon is noted. Some of the shops retain their sunshades, though it wasn't bright enough for them to be open when the modern image was taken. Troon has grown considerably, its port now a busy marina, though there are still fishing boats based there; timber is imported to the sawmill, and Irish ferries disembark from the quayside. The shipyard has gone, most employment now being based on tourism. Extensive housing estates surround the town, located between the seven golf courses. The South Woods are the location of numerous large villas and small country houses, said to be the richest part of Ayrshire.

WEST KILBRIDE

HISTORICALLY THIS VILLAGE was called Kilbride, but gradually confusion with East Kilbride in Lanarkshire resulted in the appellation 'West' being adopted around 1800. The village was famous for its early potatoes, and the arrival of the railway resulted in it being a popular watering place, with Seamill Hydropathic hotel opened in 1879 by Dr Kirk of Edinburgh, and a number of convalescent homes for various urban towns, such as Paisley, or the Scottish Co-operative Society. This view of Main Street at The Cross was taken from outside the Kilbride Tavern. The shops were large and prosperous, architecturally superior to many villages. On the left was Todd Brothers' grocery and ironmongery. Behind this was a large warehouse, four storeys in height. On the opposite side of the street stands Robert Speirs's shop. On the nepus gable is a sphere, added to the building in 1879.

AS WITH MOST small towns, the main shopping areas have suffered from the closure of shops. West Kilbride, however, has not sat back and let this happen in the same way as other communities, for it has established itself as a 'Craft Town', promoting arts and crafts, to attract tourists from near and far. As a result a number of the older commercial premises are now occupied by studios, craft shops or workshops, keeping the streets more attractive and giving the village a purpose. The large convalescent homes have gone, but Seamill Hydro Hotel continues to offer holidays by the sea. Todd's is now a branch of the Royal Bank, and the warehouse is occupied by smaller shops. On the opposite side of the street is a wool and soft toy shop. In the distance can be seen Kirktonhall House, built in 1660 but rebuilt over the years.

If you enjoyed this book, you may also be interested in…

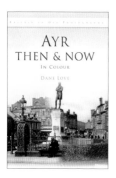

Ayr Then & Now
DANE LOVE

Ayr Then & Now takes a fond look at the Royal Burgh of Ayr over the past decades, contrasting a fascinating selection of archive photographs and postcards alongside modern photography of Ayr as it is today. From the early exploits of Sir William Wallace, through Ayr's connection to the life of Robert Burns, to more recent buildings and notable events, this is a wide-ranging look at the town, past and present.

978 0 7524 6322 3

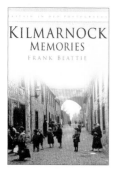

Kilmarnock Memories
FRANK BEATTIE

Until the beginning of the nineteenth century, Kilmarnock lived by what was produced locally. But after the Industrial Revolution many industries found a home in the town, producing goods from whiskey to carpets and from shoes to heavy machinery. *Kilmarnock Memories* records the growth of this Ayrshire community from its earliest origins as a sleepy village to the thriving town it has become.

978 0 7509 3236 3

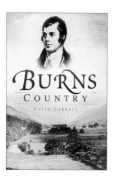

Burns Country
DAVID CARROLL

Robert Burns (1759-1796) is Scotland's most-loved poet and his words immortalised the beautiful and untamed West Coast. David Carroll's selection provides a fascinating journey through the life of Scotland's national poet, which will not only stir the memories of those people long familiar with Ayrshire and Dumfriesshire, but will also serve as an introduction to anyone exploring 'Burns Country' for themselves.

978 0 7524 4956 2

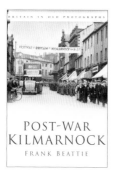

Post-War Kilmarnock
FRANK BEATTIE

Local author Frank Beattie is known for his popular local history column, 'Memories', in the *Kilmarnock Standard*, as well as having written several books on various aspects of the town's history. In his new book, Frank Beattie discusses the dramatic changes which have taken place in the decades since the Second World War. Illustrated with 250 old postcards, advertisements and ephemera, this insightful and informative book is sure to appeal to anyone who grew up in Kilmarnock or has ties with this rapidly changing town.

978 0 7509 5038 1

Visit our website and discover thousands of other History Press books.

www.thehistorypress.co.uk